MW00973652

NO WRONG WAY TO
BE A WOMAN

Kelli Gibbs

Table of Contents

Acknowledgment

Writing a book is more rewarding than I could have ever imagined. None of this would have been possible without God. For this reason, I would like to thank God for everything. In the process of putting this book together, I realized how true this gift of writing is for me. You give me the power to believe in my passion and pursue my dreams. I could never have done this without the faith I have in you.

To my mom, Geraldine Young, I can barely find the words to express the priceless wisdom, love, and support you have given me. I am eternally grateful. If I am blessed to live long enough, I hope I will be as loving, caring and giving to everyone in need.

I love you, mom.

A very special thanks to my husband, Travis Gibbs who has always been there for me. I am thankful for your hard work, love, and support in making sure that I follow and achieve my dreams.

More importantly of all, I show extensive gratitude to my nephews Corey and Codey Young for your love and support for always believing in me and helping achieve my weight loss and business goals. Without your willingness to share your knowledge, time and commitment, I wouldn't have been able to reach my goals.

Special thanks to Susan for helping to order my thoughts in making the book There is *No Wrong Way To Be A Woman* a reality. You are terrific, and I appreciate you so much.

Introduction

There is no wrong way to be a woman; neither is nature bias to have made some women and some men. But the social construct that looks beyond fairness and order have eroded the possibility of having evergreen cooperation, marred with inequality targeted at denigrating the role of women. As their duty as a woman and a mom conditions them to serve but remain unserved while their time flies with little or no consideration for self-care as they spend most of their time giving care to the loved ones while their plight to get a similar dose of attention is not considered. Empathy is the ultimate drive that spurs women to action which is the reason they love unconditionally, care unconditionally, showcasing their natural inclination to enabling a healthy household for their family.

My kids, my husband, my job; these are the universal sequence in which a woman sees the ideal role of herself which can take a slight tweak in arrangement but maintains the same selfless sequence. It has been the societal expectation of a woman since the beginning of time. Of all the listed MY's is an important, yet omitted part; **MY SELF**. Women have experienced the worse treatment when it comes to social gratitude and recognition with their immense effort completely ignored even as they remain subservient to the dictates of the social system.

Recognizing the 'self' as fundamental before the other 'MYs' is a vital step to ensuring a all- inclusive order contrary to the age-old structure where a woman is overwhelmed with the responsibility and relationship at her detriment. While a few have risen to challenge the status quo, millions are suffering in silence across every corner of the world. Worst of all the obvious is a failure to acknowledge this problem which has taken a deep plunge, courtesy of the pervasively patriarchal social construct.

As women play most of the domestic roles which permeate through every area of the society. It's no secret that our society still gives men the edge over women in lots of places such as positions of power and pay scales while women work tirelessly with less regard or appreciation which has never been given, an acknowledgment that is long expected but not offered. But it seems so little is being done to reconcile these trends. In recent times, issues with the treatment of people based on race, national origin, and sexual orientation have been key topics of discussion, but injustices by sex are usually swept under the rug. While these ills are lying unchecked, there is a consideration for self-love and self-care to bridge the gap and restore parity just so our hope and self-esteem can be restored.

Furthermore, staying organized is very vital in all areas of life! It is important to have a place of peace to go when all is said and done at the end of the day. The house serves as a sanctuary, and sorting these details out can help you get through the day, as well as be refreshed and ready for the next one. This is another significant responsibility which poses a greater threat to women's chance for self-love; **Household chores!** More consequences can be outwardly obvious to not keeping on top of certain household duties. Division of these things could also on its own cause issues, depending upon the personality types of the individuals involved. However, it is also a woman's responsibility; another reason to deny them the possible time for self-love which further narrows the chances of having one.

Another challenge is knowing how to handle your time as a woman which is the most important step to being able to juggle your different roles. Time management is extremely important in today's fast-paced society. This, however, is just one step to being able to manage your many roles as a woman today. As women's roles have begun to change, the responsibility of a woman in society can sometimes be a little unclear. If we say that her role is to bear children, some may say it is derogatory or biased – even though biologically we are the only gender who can bear children. A woman's responsibility within society is a tricky subject to pin down completely precisely because she fulfills so many different roles all at the same time. This is the reason why women need assistance, skills, inspiration, and insight to juggle the roles effectively.

However, we all have a truth that we need to live and share. For me, that truth was committing to the daily practice of repeating the phrase "I love myself." When you love yourself, life loves you back. It is not wrong to be a mom; it is not wrong to be a woman. Once we learn to consider ourselves as one who also needs love and care. There our victory lies while we struggle hard to effect a change as much as we can, the biggest changes that need to be made are not tied down to a particular field or environment - not household chores, work, family and relationship - but appear throughout the social sphere.

My Account

If marriage is your definition of happiness, mine is not. For some, beautiful houses with an in- ground pool could be their objects of happiness while expensive cars and other material stuff delight some. Yours might be spending your entire active life working on gaining your master's degree and landing your dream job. We all have individual preferences that shaped our perception of happiness. Fortunately, marriage, beautiful houses, dream job, clothing line, and other beautiful things are what I have always had, but in all my possessions, I never experienced true happiness until I made a crucial decision;

I loved myself!
My name is Kelli Gibbs, and this is my story...

Life, on my side, has always been fair right from childhood to adulthood. I was fortunate to have a caring mother who had laid my path from the beginning as I was given the best education anyone could have. My mother was a hardworking single parent that put both my older brother and me through Catholic School. Growing up was fun with less drama about life, but one thing I will always remember was my mother's endless emphasis on love for all which is about your husband, kids, and job.

My mom expressed love through cooking, rushing home every day after work and preparing a homemade dessert every day of the week. She didn't believe in eating out. We always had home cooked meals, and she was a no-nonsense woman that speaks her mind all the time.

While she radiates unconditional love, the nuances of her body language have been independence. I have always wanted to be like my mom: *to be independent and to do it all*. From my childhood, until I got married, her advice has always been my watchword.

As a obedient child who sticks to her mother's moral principle, my commitment to motherhood as taught by my mom never waver such that I do not say 'NO.' I don't think the word 'NO' was ever in my vocabulary. If I were tired after a long active day, I would keep pushing myself, working full-time, running a business, cooking, cleaning, yard work, paying bills and taking the kids to practices even on the weekends. Of all the catalog of activities, none was about myself but a effort to make others happy. I was so thoroughly selfless such that after spending money on myself, I would start feeling guilty. Lack of self-care on myself started to show as my weight spiraled out of control gaining over a hundred pounds. I felt lousy headaches, stress, and insomnia. I wanted to give up, but I pushed myself harder to put a smile on peoples' face at my detriment because I am a wife and a mom who loves all.

Of all my trove of experience some of which I learned, some of which mom taught me, there is something surprisingly amiss, something extremely significant that measures my ability to deliver the unconditional love in me, something that activates the positive energy in me that connects the ambiance in a beautiful union: God, self care and self love.

Even after I'd realized my health condition, I still make excuses fighting my inner spirit on taking the right step to freedom. March 2014 was when my story changed. It was the turning point in the story of my life. I could hear God clear as day telling me that it's time for me to take care of myself. The next day, I made an appointment with a Dr. At my appointment, the medical assistant weighed me which has always been a dreadful exercise, I had blood work and they checked my blood pressure. All the results were scary; my weight was scary, my blood pressure was alarmingly high as it reads 200/100 which was a terrifying result especially as an healthcare worker that knows the potential outcome of high blood pressure.

My physician said that I would have to take blood pressure pills. This was the final piece in my jigsaw; it was how my self-care journey began.

I signed up for a gym membership. I had this trainer that motivated me and believed in me. I had to get weighed. They checked my Body Mass Index (BMI), whoa I wasn't expecting the results to be that bad, but they truly were. The truth of the matter is just that I needed to hear it & see it on paper to make the necessary changes for me. I had lost weight in the past and gained it all back. The difference this time is that I am mentally ready to make the necessary changes in my life, and I realized that **it is not a diet but a lifestyle change.**

Through this exciting journey, I had an opportunity to reflect a lot on finding out more about me. I noticed that I am an emotional eater. I eat when I am happy, stressed, sad, or just to be eating-one of the steps I take for self-care was **discipline**; no large french fries twice a week and a large sweet tea from McDonald's and no more ice cream, or chips at night.

Now the journey officially begins. Each morning, I would go to the gym and workout for 1hr 30-minute four times a week, and I started eating healthier.

I embraced my fitness journey with utmost zest, working so hard to make the necessary change. After going to the gym for a month, that 1hr 30 minute made a significant change in me. I felt better; I had more energy going to the gym. It was such a delightful recovery mode that makes me feel excited every day. I could not remember the last time I felt so happy.

Who could ever imagine the irony of my life?

Is love not perceived to be the ultimate source of joy?

Sorry to disappoint you, It is absolutely not in my case. I have been married for seventeen years, and I have been unhappy. We had a beautiful house with an in-ground pool, expensive cars, and name brand clothes. I searched endlessly for happiness in material things, but I was wrong.

My husband, my daughter and material things have failed me woefully, so has my mother's philosophy of taking care of others without a 'me' time. I never saw my mom take care of herself which is why my journey has never been an exciting one until I switched to self-love and self-care mode. I was wrong to expect my happiness from anyone else. Ultimately, for me to be happy, it has to come from me.

Another twist to my story is the unexpected. Life is unfair as no one is too good to be tested by the damning eventualities of life. I was never prepared for what was to come. The sudden reality jolted me into another realization of life. I mentioned earlier that I had been married for years, what I didn't say is that my husband and I tried for several years to have children. I was 20 weeks with our first miscarriage. It broke my heart! I became depressed, angry and confused; my husband was torn to pieces. I never saw him broken until it happened. The miscarriage shoved us to a breaking point as we both cried for several days and became withdrawn. Two days later, the time came for the memorial service with a few family members to say goodbye to Travis Arik; I felt so numb and broken inside. I could not help my husband, neither could I help myself.

I was traumatized so much that I avoided places where there are children. Even family members would invite me to their children's birthday parties, but I could not go. My sleeping patterns were off; I would be up all night and sleep during the day. I could not get myself together. I decided after a month to see a psychiatrist despite the negative things family would say to me. Ultimately, I did what was best for me, and *where family saw me seeing a psychiatrist as a form of weakness, it became my strength. It was the best thing that I could have done for me.*

Having a prodigious support system is essential for you to achieve your ultimate goals. For me, I had my nephews Corey

& Codey whose support I immensely enjoyed. It was Corey that helped me achieve my weight loss goal. He is a personal trainer with a plethora of knowledge on how to lose weight and maintain it. I had hit a plateau, and he immediately instructed me on what to do.

Codey inspired me to become a Certified Life Coach and helped me get my life coaching business up and running which is Channel U LLC. I empower & inspire women to reconnect with themselves by channeling their passions and creativity to achieve success through one-on- one sessions, group sessions, 10-minute micro-coaching sessions, workshops, vision board socials, and wellness retreats. I specialize in stress management, self-love, healthy habits & relationship

Ladies, why do you choose to exist when you can live? Why do you choose to cope when you can flow?

Why do you have to settle when you can enjoy?

You do not deserve any less than happiness because you are special, yes, you are different Make self-care a daily regimen, and your mind, body, soul, and spirit will thank you later.

During my time of reflection, and getting to known me, I started walking four days a week. Every day that I walked I felt great. I had so much energy. I started challenging myself which was a nice experience. I loved riding my bike as a child, so do I as an adult. Riding a bike is so easy. Isn't it? (So, I thought until I messed up LOL)

I am a competitive person. I made my mind up that I would bike ten miles the first day. I was fooled Lol. I could not even cover a mile when I got tired. I am the type that does not give up.

So, I pushed myself and rode two miles that day. I went home upset and felt defeated, but the burning determination to achieve my target never wane. I was determined to achieve this the next day I biked five miles, and before I knew it, I was biking ten miles a day. My nephew Corey suggested that I need to switch my workout routine so that I will ride one day and walk the next which I did. I was walking 13 miles in a day and biking 20 miles another day. Next, I started jumping rope, a 100 jumps every other day. I have always wanted to take a Zumba class which I did, and I fell in love. I started doing Zumba twice a week, and I would walk twice a week. I also wanted to do belly dancing. I signed up for belly dancing class once a week.

Zumba is three times a week, and belly dancing one night a week. I signed up for several 5k races, and I decided to go back to school. I meditated and even tried a yoga class. I will be graduating in 4 weeks with a Bachelors in Healthcare Management.

Since my self-care began, my life has taken a new turn. I have always been happy all the time while my focus on being a mother remains intact. I focused more on myself, and I realized my family was happy the same way I am.

I am a living proof that taking time to get to know you will make a difference in your life which is why this book is written.

To ladies out there, you are never alone. We all have this spirit in us, the zest and beauty that abide in us are priceless. We have to put our self first and ensure that we never lose focus on our role as a mother and to ensure that we are always happy.

YOU FIRST!

Wonder what the ultimate steps to individual happiness are? These are highlighted below for your entertainment. Read on and enjoy... (winks)

Self-Care and Self Love

At the early stage of my motherhood was a real challenge as I juggle every role and relationships efficiently which was fun in the beginning until my strength at getting things done began to wane. For me, all I wanted to do was be the best mom, wife, and friend, to embrace the maternal role as my mom, taught me.

"First, you take care of your kid, second, you take care of your husband" This was her favorite expression. Surprisingly, there was never a third. Every time I seem to slack, my mother's voice rings like a bell in my head: a constant reminder that I use to check myself anytime I seem to falter.

Also, if I was tired I would keep pushing myself harder to get things done, like working full- time, running a business, cooking, cleaning, yard work, paying bills and taking the kids to practices even on the weekends, some I did simultaneously, some I did synchronously. I didn't make any time for myself, and once I think about spending money on myself: I would start feeling guilty. Not taking care of myself started to show as my weight had spiraled out of control gaining over a hundred pounds. I felt lousy headaches, stress, and insomnia. I felt like giving up. I still kept pushing myself and not taking time for me. Just like the way you put a smile on your face in public and work, despite your situation, and how I was feeling.

My health deteriorates further, but my mind was bent on being a good mom which was my drive right from the beginning. As a mom, it's easy to lose yourself in the day-to-day routines of family life: carpools, laundry, preparing meals, paying bills, cleaning, etc. Before you know it, ten years have gone by, and you're a shell of your former self. This is another reason we need to put our self forward, but putting yourself forward requires intentional choices especially for busy moms, even if that means stepping outside your comfort zone and putting yourself first.

But you can feel healthy, look great, and live a joyful life, all while juggling a family and a career. The key to this is designing a balanced life through purposeful choices that feed your body, mind, spirit and soul.

Also, self-love is a paradox though. In the highest reality as humans, we are Beings of Love. This is who we are in essence especially moms who are naturally chosen to conceive and share the love in the best way imaginable from pregnancy to infant stage, childhood and adulthood. These are stages a mom never gets tired of showing her love. Showering her unconditional love without getting as much in return. So if this is who we are as women, why do we need to learn 'how to' love our Self?

When I say self-love, I do not mean "likeness." Not the way you feel when you look into the mirror, not the way you feel when you land your dream job when you can fund the vacation and the endless list of material satisfactions that comes with fulfillment. Self-love, however, is a state of appreciation

for oneself that grows from actions that support our physica ,
psychological and spiritual growth. Self-love is dynamic; it
grows by actions that mature us. When we act in ways that
expand self-love in us, we begin to accept much better our
weaknesses as well as our strengths, have less need to explain
our short-comings, have compassion for ourselves as human
beings struggling to find personal meaning, are more centered
in our life purpose and values, and expect living fulfillment
through our efforts.

We Need to Love Ourselves for these Selected Reasons

You need to love yourself because self-love brings you total
awareness to the present moment of your life especially from
the endless hustle of life. And when we do not do this, we
need to shift into observation mode to discover what we are
making more important than the present moment. This is the
best way to know that we must slow down to embrace all
that arise in the present moment. You also have to be mindful
because people who have more self-love tend to know what
they think, feel and want. They are mindful of who they are
and act on this knowledge, rather than on what others want
for them.

Live

You will accept and love yourself more, whatever is happen-
ing in your life when you live with purpose and design. Your
purpose doesn't have to be crystal clear to you. If you intend
to live a meaningful and healthy life, you would make decisions that support this intention, and feel good about yourself

ucceed in this purpose. You will love yourself
see yourself accomplishing what you set out to
to establish your living intentions, to do this.

Give Priorities to Your Need Over Want

You love yourself when you can turn away from something
that feels good and exciting to what you need to stay strong,
centered, and moving forward in your life. By staying focused
on what you need, you turn away from automatic behavior
patterns that get you into trouble, keep you stuck in the past,
and lessen self-love.

Practice

By practicing Self-love, you are to be conversant with the
studies of universal laws: the Law of giving and receiving,
the law of karma: that everything that goes around will come
around, the law of attraction, the law of thinking. You should
observe these laws at work as well as your everyday life.

Positive Energy

Self-love devotes time to mastering energy release techniques
so that she can easily pivot away from her programmed mind
as quickly as possible. Self-love knows that positive energy
attracts positive energy. Self-love knows that you get what
you give. Just like karma, what goes around comes around.
Self-love also understands there may be wise things to learn
within the lower vibrations of memory and story as she works
to rise above them.

Self-Protection

—family

This can be done by bringing the right people into your life. Negative people will always find a way to pull you down. They take pleasure in your pain and loss rather than your happiness and success. These are the type of people you need to get rid of not by violence, but a calculated means of withdrawal. There isn't enough time in your life to waste on people who want to take away the delight and the shine on your face. Once you do this, you will love and respect yourself more.

Forgiveness

Another important thing is forgiveness. Try to forgive yourself as we humans can be so hard on ourselves, biting hard on things that are often time beyond our control. The downside of taking responsibility for our action is punishing ourselves too much for mistakes in learning and growing. Self-love forgives, she learns how to forgive in a way that feels aligned with her soul. She forgives herself and others. You have to accept your humanness-the the fact that you are not perfect-before you can truly love yourself. Practice being less hard on yourself when you make a mistake. Remember, there are no failures if you have learned and grown from your mistakes; there are only lessons learned to engage similar actions with experience in the future.

Illuminate Your World

Darkness is simply the absence of light. You can't push the darkness away. You can't hide from it. Similarly, you can't hide from depression, anxiety, self-hate, and more and you don't need to. The only thing you need to do is to turn the light on to let the sun shine in through the window. Whenever you feel like you are in darkness, just let light in through the window. You don't need to escape or destroy the darkness. Just let in the light.

Consciousness

Self-love knows that the body is a manifestation of her consciousness, so when her body has pain or a disturbance, she looks to the place in her consciousness that hides in the dark. Self- love invests in learning to love herself with the same excitement that she invests in a vacation or a new home. Self-love realizes that her very core is Love, that she is a being of light. Self- love makes this real in her daily life by practicing stillness.

Boundaries

You will love yourself more when you set limits or learn how to say no to work at the wrong time, love after you are shown the red flag or activities that deplete or harm you physically, emotionally and spiritually, or express poorly who you are especially about activities that are parasitic to your growth. Self-love is being consciously alert all the time to the needs for your individual development.

Cognitive Consonance

Self-love is learning to recognize the state of harmony and internal consistency arising from compatibility among your person, attitudes, your behavior, and your knowledge. Self-love is learning to recognize the story playing in your head, feel the impact and check your inner self and inquire about the truth within you.

Reading

When you read, you are practicing self-love by reading books that resonate with your knowledge and not adopting others words but allowing them to support your alignment with your words.

Support

When you reach out for support when you need to, you are also practicing self-love. You should understand that reaching out is a sign of strength and not weakness.

Ecstasy

Your excitement is superior to someone else's. Self-love follows her bliss. You learn to make this real by acting upon what brings you joy even if it means going against the opinion of others.

Reflection

Ensure you listen to your soul. This is your sanctuary, your forte. Self-love listens to her soul by bringing forth those words into the material plane, forming a relationship with your wisdom and taking responsibility for it.

If you choose a few of these self-love actions to work on, you will begin to accept and love yourself more. Just imagine how much you'll appreciate yourself when you exercise these steps to self-love. It is true that you can only love a person as much as you love yourself. If you exercise all of the actions of self-love that I describe here, you will allow and encourage others to express themselves in the same way. The more self-love you have for yourself, the better prepared you are for a healthy relationship. Even more, you will start to attract people and circumstances that support your well-being.

Self-Love and taking care of yourself is the most important thing you can be doing with your time. Self-worth is how much you value yourself, and it is tied with self-esteem because self- esteem is what we feel about ourselves. If you do not think that you have any self-worth, then simply improving self-esteem isn't enough because you won't believe it inside. You need to improve both to get results, and one way to do that is through therapy. These can create a negative feedback loop between your belief systems, and what is manifesting out into your reality. And if you are not feeling empowered from within and are predominantly experiencing a lack of inner peace, you may be out of alignment with your true self. A lack of self-love and care degrade not only your psychological state but also your physical state – and when your "cup" is empty, you are unable to give to yourself or help others as the saying goes "you cannot pour from an empty cup." So the bottom line is to strengthen your self-love muscle and learn to connect to and follow the guidance of your true self. You are part of the universal energy that creates life, and you have access to all the knowledge, power and wisdom it contains. Nothing less. The bonus to expanding yourself and growing through self-love and awareness is your change of state – you will be operating at a level that has a ripple effect on everyone and everything on this planet. Self-love is to know you are responsible for discerning what is loving or worthy to you, knowing that no one else can tell you what, that only God, the creator of the universe can guide you to the next moment of enlightenment filled with love.

Independence and Strength

Everyone has their perception of independence, but true independence is shaped by experience you have overtime that accumulates together and shaped your thought processes. My definition of an independent individual is a person that takes care of their responsibilities and decisions. Whenever the word INDEPENDENCE is spoken, the next word that comes to mind is 'MOM' because the experience I had while growing up and those I have as a mother have changed the narrative such that the word INDEPENDENT is synonymous with MOM. Everybody has a little thing to say when it comes to their mothers, so do I. But this time, not as a parent, but as a person who took life by its horns and paved a way. Just looking at her deal with decisions and sometimes even mistakes made me realize what strength is. My mother was a hardworking single parent that put both my older brother and me through Catholic School. I learned from my mother very early in life on how to be a strong independent woman. Everyone would like to be a mentally strong person, but mental resilience can be extremely hard to achieve when life gets on top of you not only as a woman but as a mom with loads of responsibilities. It is said that to be mentally strong, you must prevent yourself from getting carried away by emotions to the point where you can't see logic. An opinion that is incoherent with the role of motherhood where emotions overrides logic at a time, balanced at other time and often, mom's nurturing touch is a major piece of what shapes us into who we are. In a world where women are becoming more empowered and more independent, I watched my mother demonstrate these qualities with her sense of independence and strength through both minor and major life changes.

Yes, it may be hard but believe me, it is achievable. I am saying this as a daughter as well as a mother: my assertion on this is coming from three-stage experiences that span through childhood, adulthood, and motherhood. The ability to be independent is something that not everyone possesses but is achievable. You need to be independent to survive in the world.

Learning to support yourself is fundamental for any success you ever hope to achieve because if self-reliance exists in you, you can often understand the struggle of asking someone for help. Even if you are piled high with work, and you are desperate for resources, you contemplate the idea that asking for help would unease that individual.

Though you may be able to complete the task on your own, and a helping hand can create a quality product and increase relations. Truth is people enjoy helping one another. As an independent person, you can complete tasks on your own if need be. You can also put 100% in whatever you do and can take charge in the situations presented. You only have yourself to fall back on, so it is exceedingly important to be able to handle things on your own. It is all about being secure with who you are and what you believe in. It is extremely empowering knowing that you are in control of your own life and your own choices. It is much more beneficial to listen to the voice inside yourself rather than the berating opinions of others.

However, people are unable to be independent for different reasons, with fear at the forefront, the fear of being alone, the fear of rejection and the fear of the future. As you get older, you need to learn how to make the best decisions that allow you to live your lives the way you want. Developing into an autonomous person can be one of the most worthwhile outcomes you can strive for yourselves. Another essential thing to know is that there is no reason to base your life decisions on relationships with people. All relationships end at some point or another, it is the reality of life. There is nothing you can do to change that. The only thing you can do is change your perception of relationships. Instead of expecting them to make you happy by being in your life and providing enjoyment, appreciate the time spent on enjoyment since you know it will be gone at one point. To avoid sudden disappointment, you must depend on you for your happiness. The ability to be happy regardless of being in a relationship is an amazing attribute. Be mindful of that! People continue to wallow in detrimental relationships because they are scared of being on their own when in fact they are to relish it and spend the time focusing on making themselves better.

Independence From Mother to Child

Education

Very early in my life, I was raised to value education because it is the first thing on my mother's list. If there is one person I have to thank for my education, it's her, my knight in the shiny armor. It was not something imposed, neither was I compelled, but her diligence at getting her job done left me with no other example to follow. At first, I got antsy, the usual childhood angst but over time, my irritation changed to intrigue. Our education has always been her priority. My mother believes the only way to face the world with the right energy is getting an education, and she left no stone unturned she sometime gets back late from work but still stays up late with me till I get my work done. She was always there, helping and guiding at every turn.

Unconditional Love

This is an indescribable aspect of motherhood that never wanes. This is not the love that is learned or taught but the natural affection that arose from a unique bond between a mother and her child. No matter how much we fought, or how strict she got, or how much I thought I could not live under the same roof with her, she remains my last resort, my shield, my confidant, my irresistible beacon of hope on a stormy day. She was always there till adulthood when I was rife with raging hormones. She showered me with endless love even when I was craziest. She is the only one I turned to when the night was darkest. The care to eat, the persuasion to ensure I do not go to bed angry as well as the entreating gestures of delights. I wonder what I have done to deserve her.

Security

Ladies, one important thing to know is that security for your kids is crucial to their independence because toddlers and children will naturally become independent if they are raised in an environment where they feel secure. This fear is quite understandable considering the security situation of our present society. It starts when they are very young. The first time you leave your toddler's sight, and they experience separation is a milestone for them. By being aware of your children's security needs and guiding them through separation issues in a positive way; you will help them develop a sense of security. That's the first of many steps in your child becoming independent.

Assistance

Asking for help with small tasks is one step you can take to help encourage your child's independence. You can begin to do this at a young age. You can ask them to help clean the family car, you can ask them to help with laundry, and they can also walk the dog or some task in the courtyard.

Prayer

This is an important aspect of parenting that every lady must know and put to practice. Either you are a staunch believer or a passive one, you need to guide your kids the spiritual way to set their path from the beginning. Faith is the believe you have in what you cannot see, but the moral sense that comes with spirituality is enough to guide your kids from childhood to adulthood. My mom was a good example: her faith is all you need to see to remain positive and independent in life and with confidence, she also showed me the importance of gratitude. Her gratitude to God taught me that nobody owes you a thing. So, be grateful even if the act of kindness was a lent dollar in a time of need.

Courage

As a woman, your kids must be raised to be courageous. My mom warned that nothing was supposed to bring me down. Not bad grades, heartbreaks, **Nothing!**. I have seen her mourn the losses of friends failed to get things done, seen her at her lowest but I never see her give up on life. There is always the courage to rise and move on. She starts a new day with new energy leaving the past in the past while she concentrates only in the present and hopes for the best in the future. This is an important lesson I learned that you also should adopt. You can mourn, but you cannot make mourning your life. So, stand up once again and face your challenges head-on.

Mistakes

This is a crucial aspect of development for humanity in general either old or young. It is the measure of performance to help us know if we are progressing or retrogressing especially when we retrospect on previous actions. Mistakes are what enables us to desist from the wrong by choosing the right. Ladies, you should allow children to experience natural consequences. This type of parenting will enable them to feel comfortable taking charge of their lives and becoming independent. Allow them to make mistakes because once they realize it is normal to be wrong, their dependence will take a hit and realize they are capable of handling things and making some decisions on their own.

Teach

This is where many of us are getting it wrong. This is our responsibility and not someone else's. We are our kid's guide, their teacher and their window into the vast and complex human world when we take time to train them on tasks, their sense of independence develops. You can also do this by identifying new tasks for your child per week. You can divide the task into steps and guide the child through. This may look so simple, but it helps our kids to develop a sense of confidence.

Independence from Kids to Mothers

Gratitude

This is an essential knowledge to pass across to the children. Gratitude is not an instinct; it has to be learned. We have to be a good example to the kids by thanking them often. We can also explain to them why they are being praised so they will learn the value of an action and the consequence of such good action as gratitude. Ladies, try to instill the spirit of appreciation in your kids right from their tender age as it enables them to appreciate simple act of kindness when they get one.

According to a renowned researcher, Dr. Robert Emmons who is the world's leading scientific expert on gratitude. He conducted studies involving gratitude journals and found that when people regularly engage in gratitude, they experience measurable psychological, physical, and interpersonal benefits. They:

Feel better about their lives overall
Experience higher levels of positive emotions like optimism, enthusiasm, love, and happiness Are kinder and more generous to others

Have fewer physical problems including pain Exercise more regularly and eat healthier Sleep well
Visit the doctor more regularly for checkups Feel less stressed
Able to cope with stress more effectively and recover more quickly from stressful situations
Live longer on average, being thankful adds seven years to our lives!

Curiosity

Curiosity is an essential trait of a genius which can be displayed by children at the early stage of their life. Curious children always ask questions while their mind is constantly active. You do not have to bark orders or restrict this fantastic trait but create time out of your busy schedule to attend to them. These questions might sound stupid and meaningless to you-an adult-but it means everything to them because they will only ask questions within the scope of their knowledge which may be pointless in the adult world. Hey, that is why we are there to guide them right.

Respect

Just like mirrors, children reflect us everything we say or do. Every word we hear, everything we experience, is permanently recorded in our subconscious. Whenever adults speak, we are role models for the children in our presence. What we speak is what we teach. Children record every word we ever say to them or in front of them. The language children grow up hearing is the language they will speak. This is why we must be mindful of the language we speak and practice good virtues by ourselves to be a good model for our children.

There is a different way of showing respects. Respect can mean any of these:

Having regard for others.
Having proper respect for yourself. Not interfering with others property
To consider something worthy of high regard.
When they live with disrespect, they learn disrespect.

Ladies, I need you to know that learning to support yourself is fundamental for any success you ever hope to achieve. Independent people don't rely on other people to do their jobs, but they find excessive attention annoying and offensive. Make decisions by and for yourself, whatever they may be. Do what you wanted and learn from your own mistakes. Many people are afraid to think for themselves because of that involves taking responsibility for their own lives. This is just one way people become dependent. We are born alone, and we die alone, so we each have to take responsibility for our lives at every step along the way.

Meditation and Mindfulness

Hey, Do you wish to avoid the drama and become a calm mom?

You love your kids, but sometimes they drive you crazy?

You are so worried you do not spend enough time with your kids?

Job responsibilities, chores and roles all crashing on you at once?

You feel drained by the battle to balance everything, and you feel you are losing it all?

You so wish your life could be peaceful?

If your battle is one of the barrage of questions above, you need this read, but if it is more than two, you need it more. So, you are welcome; I am here to help you. Isn't that why the book is written in the first place? (Winks) Mom and busy ladies who have been pushed to the edge of insanity by life itself need to live, or at least be free from the burden nature has placed on us as women.

You probably have heard about meditation before or you have tried too many times without success to meditate. Yes, you are not the only one dear, it happens to many of us women. Unlike the usual misconception about the act, meditation is simply the practice of turning your attention to a single point of reference. It can involve focusing on the breath, on bodily sensations, or a word or phrase known as a **mantra**. In other words, meditation means pivoting away from distracting thoughts and focusing on the present moment. People who meditate consistently find that there are short-term and long-term benefits. The goal of meditation is to focus and understand your mind, eventually reaching a higher level of awareness and inner calm. Meditation is an ancient practice, but scientists are still discovering all of its benefits.

Also, Neurologists have found that regular meditation changes your brain in ways that can help you to control emotions, enhance concentration, decrease stress, and even become more connected to those around you.

Isn't this what all we ladies crave?

With practice, you'll be able to achieve a sense of tranquility and peace no matter what's going on around you. There are many different ways to meditate, so if one practice doesn't seem to work for you before you give up consider trying a different type that works better for you.

There is no going back now that you found an antidote to your daily drama. What you should do is to make plans to actualize the steps to mindfulness.

Hey, you have no reason to quit!

The key to developing a successful meditation practice is finding the right fit for you. To figure out what kind of meditation works best for you, you'll have to put a few types of meditation to the test and try several tools so you can choose the practice that makes you comfortable.

How to Meditate

Meditation is a very simple practice that people overcomplicate. The basic idea of meditation is simple. Every time your mind begins to shift its spotlight away from your breath, and you get lost in thought, you bring your attention back to your breath. It is human nature for the mind to wander. Do not try and stop your thoughts or blank your mind. However, these tips are not aimed at making you an expert but to help you get started and keep you going. You don't have to implement them all at once. Just take one step at a time.

Find a peaceful environment

Meditation should be practiced in a peaceful location. A tranquil environment will enable you to focus exclusively on the task at hand and avoid external stimuli and distractions. Find a place where you will not be interrupted for the duration of your meditation, whether it lasts 5 minutes or half an hour. Space does not need to be very large as long as you have privacy.

Make it your first thing in the morning

It's easy to say, "I'll meditate every day when it is possible to forget. Instead, set a reminder for every morning when you get up or put a note on your wall where you can see it immediately you wake up from the bed.

Start like a beginner you are

Find something to sit on, either a chair, meditation cushion, or meditation bench. Sit for just two minutes. This will seem very easy, to meditate for two minutes. That's perfect. Start with just two minutes a day for a week. If that goes well, increase by another two minutes and do that for a week. If all goes well, by increasing just a little at a time, you'll be meditating for 10 minutes a day in the 2nd month, which is amazing! But start small first.

Put on comfortable clothes

One of the major goals of meditation is to calm the mind and block out external distractions. This can be difficult if you feel physically uncomfortable due to tight or restrictive clothing. Try to wear loose clothing during meditation practice and make sure to remove your shoes.

A timer

I suggest you use your phone but make sure to turn your phone's notification off before you begin meditating. Pretty much every phone has a timer built-in, and if you have a smartphone, chances are there is an excellent meditation app for it too.

How to sit

The biggest thing to remember is to keep your back straight keep your back erect and keep an upright posture. This keeps you alert and allows you to concentrate more easily on your breath. Your eyes can either be opened or closed. Again, the goal of this whole meditation thing is to work out your attention muscle. If you find you can concentrate better on your breath with your eyes closed, as many people do, then it's probably best to keep them closed. If you are tired and find yourself dozing off when you close your eyes, try opening them slightly and focus your gaze softly on a space on the floor in front of you. The biggest point I will like to make is about how to sit to find a posture that is comfortable and keep you upright.

The biggest thing to remember is to keep your back straight keep your back erect and keep an upright posture. This keeps you alert and allows you to concentrate more easily on your breath. Your eyes can either be opened or closed. Again, the goal of this whole meditation thing is to work out your attention muscle. If you find you can concentrate better on your breath with your eyes closed, as many people do, then it's probably best to keep them closed. If you are tired and find yourself dozing off when you close your eyes, try opening them slightly and focus your gaze softly on a space on the floor in front of you. The biggest point I will like to make is about how to sit to find a posture that is comfortable and keep you upright.

Focus on your breath

This is what meditation is all about, and it is what makes meditation both difficult and worthwhile. In this step, close your mouth and focus entirely on your breath as it enters and leaves your nose. You can focus on any element of your breath that you want. Either how the air feels as it enters and exits your nose or how the air feels as you inflate and deflate your lungs, to the sensation under your nose as you breathe in and out, to the sound you make as you breathe. You do not have to force your breathing-just to breathe naturally and observe the tranquil breath without thinking too much about it.

Do not think

This aspect is the hardest part. Don't analyze your breath; bring your attention and focus to your breath, without thinking about it or analyzing it.

Mindful of your attention

Bring your attention back whenever it wanders, slowly and calmly. When your mind wanders, gently bring your attention back to your breath once you realize that your mind has wandered. You may not clue in at first that your mind has started thinking again, but when you do, gently bring your attention back. Don't be hard on yourself during this stage. Gently bring your attention back.

Be easy on yourself

When your mind wanders, it is easy to become frustrated with yourself but don't. Your meditations will be much more productive when you gently bring your attention back.

Count your breath

If you find it hard to concentrate, try to count. Count your breaths, until you reach five, and then start again. I use this trick when I'm having a tough time concentrating.

Create a mantra

These are words you repeat silently that aid your focus on your attention during meditation. You can choose any word you like. *"love," "passion," "joy," "beauty," "happiness."* These are good suggestions for you.

Be fulfilled

When you're finished with your session, smile. Be grateful that you had this time to yourself that you stuck with your commitment, that you showed yourself that you're trustworthy, where you took the time to get to know yourself and make friends with yourself. That's an amazing moment of your life.

Meditation isn't always easy or even peaceful. But it has amazing benefits, and you can start today, and continue for the rest of your life. **Yes, you can!**

Why We Meditate

- There are numerous reasons why we meditate. Here is a few reasons we do. People who meditate:

- Experience less stress and anxiety

- They build a stronger relationship with their children

- They feel less overwhelmed by the demands of motherhood Their children experience less stress and anxiety

- Experience soothing moments of peace and calm in your busy-mom days Feel at ease and nurtured instead of feeling exhausted

- Have tender and gentle interactions with your kids instead of rash and angry ones.

Benefits of Meditation and Mindfulness

Less Stress

Meditation is a natural stress reliever, and there's no esoteric reason behind it. Scientific studies have shown that meditation can positively regulate the area of the brain that controls stress, known as the subiculum area of the hippocampus.

Improves Self Control

Scientific studies have shown that meditation is effective at improving self-control and introspection and it decreases participant's impulsivity.

Healthier Blood Pressure

A study at Harvard Medical School found that meditation lowered blood pressure by reducing the stress response, with effectiveness practically equal to that achieved using blood pressure pharmaceuticals.

Increased Compassion

When you are calm with yourself, and you are in absolute control of your emotion, you are bound to share more love than hate, positives than negatives.

Pain relief

Patients reported sharp decreases in painful symptoms following a regular practice of relaxation methods, according to a study in the Journal of Behavioral Medicine. The patients in the study – suffering from a backache, chronic migraine, tension headaches, and similar conditions – were able to lessen or, in some cases stop altogether, their use of pain drugs.

Eating Disorder

One challenge that gave me a much headache was a eating disorder. It took me so long to admit this because I focused more on others while I didn't create time for myself. Not taking care of me started to show, my weight had spiraled out of control gaining over a hundred pounds. I felt lousy headaches, stress, and insomnia. I felt like giving up. I still kept pushing myself and not taking time for me. I understand the consequences quite well because I have been working in healthcare for several years taking care of everyone else. Just how you put a smile on your face in public and work despite your situation, and how I was feeling. Eating disorders are complicated psychological conditions that affect a person's physical and emotional health. They involve intense emotions and behaviors about food. Eating disorders are very dangerous illnesses and can lead to permanent physical and psychological consequences if left untreated. People with eating disorders eat too little or too much. Extreme eating or dieting is not a normal or healthy part of being a woman. Some eating disorders also involve people making themselves throw up or taking laxatives to get rid of the food, or extreme exercise to burn off the calories. All eating disorders are dangerous if left untreated.

There are three major types of eating disorder:

1. **Anorexia Nervosa**
2. **Bulimia**
3. **Binge Eating Disorder**

These are serious mental health condition that can happen to anyone but is much common in women; **YOU READ THAT RIGHT, W-O-M-E-N!**

Although eating disorders revolve around eating and body weight, they are often more about control, feelings, and self-expression than they are about food. Women with eating disorders often use food and dieting as ways of coping with life's stress. For some, food becomes a source of comfort and nurturing, or a way to control or release stress. For others, losing weight may start as a way to gain the approval of friends and family. Eating disorders are not diets; they are signs of personal weakness or problems that will not go away without proper treatment. Most of us ladies mistake this for good health when, in fact, we are dying in silence.

Anorexia Nervosa

This is a disorder in which patients do not lose their appetite, but they struggle to subdue it which leads to excessive weight loss. If you suffer from this disease, you may not acknowledge that weight loss or restricted eating is a problem, and you may "feel fat" even when you're emaciated.

Bulimia

Women with this disorder regularly and sometimes secretly binge on large quantities of food between 2,000 to 5,000 calories at a time followed by an intense feeling of guilt and then exercise excessively or purge by self-inducing vomiting, using laxatives, enemas, or diuretics in an attempt to avoid gaining weight.

Binge Eating Disorder

It involves eating an unusually large amount of food in a short period and feeling a loss of control during this episode. People with binge eating disorder do not purge afterward, but often feel shame or guilt about their binge eating.

Causes of Eating Disorders

Lack of self-love

You are likely to find yourself in one of this eating disorder situation if you are too obsessed with taking care of others while your health means nothing to you. Busy moms and working ladies are very likely to fall into this category.

Grief

People are likely to lose people they care about a lot. Mourning can take away your appetite and restricting food or purging can be a way to deal with the feeling of losing someone.

Divorce

Also, to grief and lack of self-love, the breakup of marriage can spur a woman to view her body unfavorably in comparison with other singles or an ex-spouse's new girlfriend.

Heartbreaks

This is another form of loss that can lead to disorder in eating. Heartbreak can spur unnecessary appetite or reduced appetite significantly.

Treating Eating Disorders

Getting a diagnosis is only the first step towards recovery from an eating disorder. Treating a eating disorder generally involves a combination of psychological and nutritional counseling, along with medical and psychiatric monitoring. Treatment must address the eating disorder symptoms and medical consequences, as well as psychological, biological, interpersonal, and cultural forces that contribute to or maintain the eating disorder. Eating disorder treatment also involves addressing other health problems caused by an eating disorder, which can be serious or even life-threatening if they go untreated for too long. If a eating disorder does not improve with standard treatment, you may need hospitalization or another type of inpatient program.

Psychotherapy

This is the cornerstone of treatment for eating disorders. Various kinds of psychotherapy can help. Cognitive behavioral therapy (CBT) challenges unrealistic thoughts about food and appearance and helps people develop more productive thought patterns.

Nutritional Rehabilitation

A dietitian or nutritional counselor can help a woman recovering from an eating disorder learn or relearn the components of a healthy diet and can help motivate her to make the needed changes. At different stages in recovery, a nutrition professional will help plan how and when the patient should eat in a way that keeps the digestive system working well and avoids dangerous changes in electrolyte and fluid balances that can occur when a person begins eating again after a period of semi-starvation.

Hospitalization

Eating disorders are usually treated on a outpatient basis. But hospitalization may be recommended if a woman is dangerously underweight, unable to eat or stop vomiting, seriously depressed or suicidal, medically unstable (for example, because of heart arrhythmias, low pulse or blood pressure, or electrolyte imbalances), or has other medical complications that require hospital treatment.

Though, the road to recovery from an eating disorder, is often a difficult and challenging experience. However, there is hope in finding freedom from these illnesses. While the eating disorder treatment process may be extended and ongoing, the recovery journey is priceless because it will help you regain your life back. Nothing is more precious or valuable than your own life, your well-being. This worth every steps of the way through the process of recovery. This step is crucial for everyone suffering from one of the disorders mentioned above. You are the mom that gives care: you deserve better.

Self-Acceptance

Have you ever felt like you've never been the right type of woman?
Have you ever been judged by others at some point in your life?
Have you ever experienced any form of abuse that occupies the darkest part of your mind?
What message of condemnation have you heard from the society that has made you withdrawn from being a happy woman you used to be?

All the questions I listed above are the consequences of low self-acceptance without which our psychological well-being can suffer because we develop our self-esteem, in part, from others appreciating us or unhappy childhood where parents (or other significant people such as teachers) were extremely critical, poor academic performance in school resulting in a lack of confidence and many more. However, when we practice self-acceptance, we're able to embrace all facets of ourselves, not just the positive but also the less satisfying parts. As such, self- acceptance is unconditional, free of any qualification. We can recognize our weaknesses and limitations, but this awareness in no way interferes with our ability to accept ourselves fully.

We can define self-acceptance as an individual's acceptance of their attributes, positive or negative. It includes body acceptance, self-protection from negative criticism, and believing in one's capacities. Self-acceptance is so important because if you do not accept yourself for who you are, you will create some problems in your life. Some of these problems are internal, affecting you personally, and some will affect how others treat you. Many people fall into the trap of not accepting who they are and then try to be like someone else which can be as a result of:

- Low self-esteem
- Living a lie
- Unhappiness
- Low self-confidence
- Victim of judgment

Self-acceptance is about embracing yourself as you are right now, regardless of your past. Self- awareness plays a big role in self-acceptance. As you develop the ability to gain knowledge about yourself, you will become more and more able to accept and improve those areas where you lack confidence.

Self-acceptance takes some work. You have to be able to get to a place where you know and understand who you are, and that means that you will likely have to make some changes. Self- acceptance also means that you may have to face some fears and step outside of your comfort zone. It's about being able to separate who you are from what you've done. It's about understanding that everyone makes mistakes, and that's how we learn and grow.

Accepting yourself doesn't necessarily mean liking every aspect of yourself. That will come later, with self-love. It means being willing and able to experience everything you think, feel, or do, even if you don't always like it. If you don't accept yourself, you will feel ashamed or embarrassed about who you are.

Some of the causes of self-acceptance is not being accepted or loved unconditionally as a child. People who experienced that pain will go through life being internally motivated to compensate for that lack of acceptance by seeking it in their relationships with other people.

Also, If the most important people in your life do not accept you as you are, or they are trying to change you this will have a great impact on your level of self-acceptance. Some people with low self-acceptance try to bolster it by accomplishing great things. But this only helps your self-esteem for a while. That's because achievement is a poor substitute for intimacy. This type of people find it hard to believe in genuine caring, and when it comes their way, they are suspicious of it.

Accepting yourself and your life begins with changing your mindset to be happy. As Robert Holden puts it in his book Happiness Now! "Happiness and self-acceptance go hand in hand. Your level of self-acceptance determines your level of happiness. The more self-acceptance you have, the more happiness you'll allow yourself to accept, receive and enjoy. In other words, you enjoy as much happiness as you believe you're worthy of."

These are ways to learn to accept yourself and your life:

- Take time to think about who you are – your personality, your background and things that make you hard on yourself.

- Surround yourself with positive people that believe in you and support your goals and dreams.

- Recognizing how other people's comments affect you. Remove yourself from people who bring you down. Surround yourself with like-minded people.

- Focus on the present, and the future. Forgive yourself and move on to grow, and accept that you can't change the past.

- Understand that there are both positive and negative aspects of who you are and you should accept these as part of who you are

- Are there things about yourself which you don't like? Ok, maybe you can improve, but first acknowledge them and accept them

- Practice daily affirmations to quiet your inner critic. Challenge yourself when your inner critic tells you negative remarks. Practice catching these negative thoughts when they come up then ask yourself would you say those things to a friend that you love. Replace those with expressions like:
  I am destined for greatness.
  I am Imperfectly perfect.

I am beautiful.

- Practice gratitude by writing a handwritten letter to someone that has made a difference in your life telling them that you appreciate them. You can hand deliver it or mail it.

- Make a list and acknowledge your strengths and attributes. Recognizing your strengths will help you learn about yourself.

Without self-acceptance, your psychological well-being can suffer, and often, beneficial interventions are less helpful for you than for others with higher self-acceptance. If you accept yourself, you can also value yourself and tell others that they should respect who you are. Self- acceptance is reciprocal because you will also be able to accept others and not demand that they try to reach your standards. You will also be able to ask others for what you want and need.

Self-acceptance means that you are happy with who and what you are, but it does not mean that you give up any hopes of change or improvement. Self-acceptance is a necessary first step towards self-improvement because you need to see the truth about yourself and accept it and then decide whether or, not you can change.

Ladies, this is what we want. Our happiness is our responsibility. By accepting our flaws and shortcomings as part of our being, we'll be closer to ultimate mental satisfaction with ourselves than we could imagine. Let's put the tips for self-acceptance into practice right away for absolute joy that we deserve.

Joy of Motherhood

This is the duty that unites us all, regardless of race, religion, background, a duty that gives us an immeasurable sense of fulfillment, completing the circle of love that enriches all of humankind, as new life adds to the rich tapestry of humanity in its unique way. It is a experience every lady will give their all to have, an unchangeable responsibility of adaptation on the female sex since the beginning of time. Mother is not simply a word, but it is a whole universe in itself. She is the most important person in everybody's life. As God cannot be everywhere, he created MOTHER. Despite the obvious consequences-the apparent challenges that trail motherhood-women are willing to risk their own lives to bring a child into the world. It is the greatest sacrifice one person can make for another. It is the deepest form of love there ever is.

How can we define motherhood? What does it means to be a mother? These questions are as challenging to answer as they are simple. To give birth? Yes, to adopt children? Yes! To have a family? Yes! But being a mother is much more than that. There are some large, overwhelming, and beautiful piece at the center of motherhood that is so hard to put words to them. It's a feeling, not a explanation. Maybe that piece is best-called love. If so, it is truly a unique love reserved for the mother/child relationship. And when you've felt it, you know it. Motherhood is one of the most difficult jobs there is. It marks a new chapter in every woman's story. It gives you a new strength in yourself, something you didn't know was there until you had children. It also gives you a new sense of purpose and meaning in life. You encounter love and passion for your children that you've never experienced before.

Motherhood is cleaning up messes. It's wiping down kitchens after cooking meals and preparing snacks all day long. Washing floors spotted with muddy footprints from exploring all day and cleaning windows smudged with tiny fingerprints. It's wiping runny noses from sick babies and drying tears from your toddler after a nightmare.

Motherhood is amazing. It's looking into your child's eyes and seeing nothing but love. It's watching them evolve and grow into tiny people with their unique personalities. It is spending sleepless nights worrying about them, agonizing over their health and safety. It is stumbling out of a warm bed at 2 AM to make sure your child is still breathing. It is changing our bodies for our kids. Motherhood is watching as our belly stretches and grows, never to return to its original form. It is about postponing runs and gyms occasionally so that we could stay in bed and snuggle with them a little longer.

However, as mothers, we shouldn't aim for perfection, but instead, develop traits that create healthy relationships for ourselves and our kids. Motherhood is a journey where we can develop the kind of traits in ourselves we would want to see in our kids.

Tips for becoming the best mom

Life is beautiful as a mother. My life is a total and utter blessing. My life is constantly busy, messy, hectic, and often focused on meeting the needs of others. I am a mom. A full-time working mom. I have been working in healthcare for several years taking care of everyone else both at home and at work. I wake up every morning, long before my kids flutter an eyelash so that I can shower, dress, get breakfast ready, and enjoy a cup of hot tea before my caregiving mode is switched on. Overtime, motherhood has been more of a blessing to me because I have made a significant success juggling both responsibilities. (work and mother). Some of the tips below are what I did which I know will help you too.

Empathetic

This is about showing an ability to understand and share the feelings of another. Responding to your child with empathy makes you wonder why they behaved the way they did instead of launching into full discipline mode. By doing this, you are likely to calm things down than exacerbate them. The next time your child throws a tantrum, calm them down with a pleasant word or remark to let them know it is normal as a kid to get mad sometime. Try this, and you will gain more control over them.

Patience

Patience is very crucial in parenting. When we are patient, we're less likely to yell: we won't lose our temper or say things we can regret. It is normal to feel frustrated to a breaking point. Once this happens, you should either take a break or slowdown from unnecessary stress. With an adequate level of patience, we are likely to react in a more controlled way to issues that are mischievous.

Communication

This is a classic motherhood skill that we ignore at our peril. The importance of communication cannot be overemphasized. Ask why your child is behaving in a certain way. Chances are, an underlying reason you haven't even thought about is lurking beneath. Think of what they must be feeling and put yourself in their shoes for a better understanding.

Love and Praise

Mothers truly understand the power of positive praise and encouragement versus criticism or silence. Either your kids are right or wrong, ensure you praise first before you criticize. This is very crucial to their confidence, and it will influence their way of handling issues. Remember our children are like a mirror that gives back exactly what we give to them.

Authoritative

A good mom knows how to be responsive and nurturing, but also show authority and sets high expectations. Kids need boundaries so they can explore within safe confines. As a mother, we have to support our kids as they learn and grow. Set your expectations for them so they won't be confused as to what is needed to be done. Above all, your authority should not stop them from making choices because it helps them take ownership of their actions.

Respect

Treating your child with respect is the bedrock of their relationship with others in society. It is a mistake to think your child is too young to know what respect is. Right from toddlerhood to childhood, they deserve full respect. Respect, your child for being the unique person they are, not an extension of you. They are a wonderful, independent person with a budding personality and their tastes, likes, and dislikes, wants and needs.

Humility

No one is above mistake. We are not infallible, and we should not try to behave like we are. We can't expect kids to own up to their own mistakes if we never do so to ours. We need to model how to make mistakes. Be gracious and humble and your kids will too.

Fun and Laughter

You might be finding it difficult to cope, but the truth is, parenting is fun. Breathe and enjoy every moment with your bundle of joy and do not forget to smile.

Pray

Above everything, you need to guide your kids spiritually. Pray for them and teach them how to pray. This is a journey where all form of strength is needed both physical, psychological and spiritual.

Mothers will, for the rest of our lives, wear our hearts on our sleeves. We will bend without breaking. We will scream and cry because we need a break from our babies and then miss them as soon as we are gone. We will realize that all of the worry and sacrifice and time was worth it. We will come to understand that all of the things we've done for them doesn't compare to what they have done for us. Much love to give and so much more to be given in return.

This is a brief insight into our world. Busy ladies and mothers deserve all form of happiness there is. This is the beginning of a journey I hope we will embark together. As this little piece of advice is given, **more is yet to come**.

Honestly, there is no wrong way to be a woman.

NEVER!

Q1

What do you like
about yourself?

678 301 6125

Made in the USA
Columbia, SC
02 April 2019